ELEPHANTS
PAST AND PRESENT

MARIANNE JOHNSTON

The Rosen Publishing Group's

PowerKids Press™

New York

Published in 2000 by The Rosen Publishing Group, Inc.
29 East 21st Street, New York, NY 10010

First Edition

Book Design: Michael deGuzman, Resa Listort, Danielle Primiceri

Photo Credits: pp. 1, 7, 20, 22 © 1997 Digital Vision Ltd; ; pp. 1, 7, 8, 11, 12, 16, 19 © Dr. Adrian Lister; pp. 3,5 © 1996 PhotoDisc, Inc.; p. 5 © Jonathan Blair/Corbis, 1996 Andromeda Interactive Ltd.; p. 10 © Ray Colby/Potomac Museum; p. 15 © Michael Maslan Historic Photographs/Corbis; p. 15 © Super Stock; p. 19 © Corbis-Bettmann.

Johnston, Marianne.
     Elephants past and present / by Marianne Johnston.
          p.   cm.—(Prehistoric animals and their modern-day relatives)
     Includes index.
     Summary: Discusses the prehistoric relatives, evolution, and modern species of elephants.
     ISBN 0-8239-5202-9
     1. Elephants, Fossil—Juvenile literature. 2. Elephants—Juvenile literature. [1. Elephants, Fossil. 2. Elephants. 3. Prehistoric animals.] I. Title. II. Series: Johnston, Marianne. Prehistoric animals and their modern-day relatives.
     QE882.P8J65 1998
     569'.67—dc21   98-3877
                                                                                                        CIP
                                                                                                        AC

Manufactured in the United States of America

CONTENTS

HISTORY OF THE ELEPHANT

Elephants and their **ancestors** have walked Earth for millions of years. These intelligent, powerful, and gentle creatures have an amazing history.

Over the past 45 million years, almost 150 **species** of elephants and their relatives have lived and died. The great **mastodons** and **mammoths**, along with other early elephant-like creatures once lived on every continent except Australia and Antarctica.

Only two species of elephants live on Earth today. ▶

ELEPHANT EVOLUTION

All animals that have trunks like elephants are called **proboscideans**. The very first of these animals lived about 45 million years ago. That was after most of the dinosaurs had already become **extinct**. The first proboscideans looked a lot like pigs.

Over the course of millions of years, these animals went through a slow process of change and development, called **evolution**. Many animals and plants go through the process of evolution. Some species don't evolve, or **adapt**, to nature's changes and they become extinct.

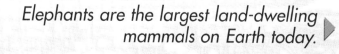

Elephants are the largest land-dwelling mammals on Earth today. ▶

EARLY ELEPHANTS

The first elephant-like creature that lived was only about the size of a pig. **Moeritherium** lived 40 million years ago and looked kind of like a mini-hippopotamus. It lived near water like hippos do. It didn't have much of a trunk, but it did have the very beginnings of tusks.

About 15 million years later, another kind of early elephant had evolved. **Deinotherium** was thirteen feet tall and looked a lot like a modern-day elephant. Instead of having tusks that pointed forward, Deinotherium's short tusks curved back toward its neck.

Tusks keep growing in size as an animal gets older. ▶

CLOSER RELATIVES OF THE ELEPHANT

A third group of early elephants evolved along with the other **prehistoric** elephant-like creatures. This group, known as the early modern elephants, would lead directly to modern elephants.

One member of this branch was *Elephas falconeri*. This **dwarf** elephant lived about 5 million years ago on islands in the Mediterranean Sea near what is now Greece.

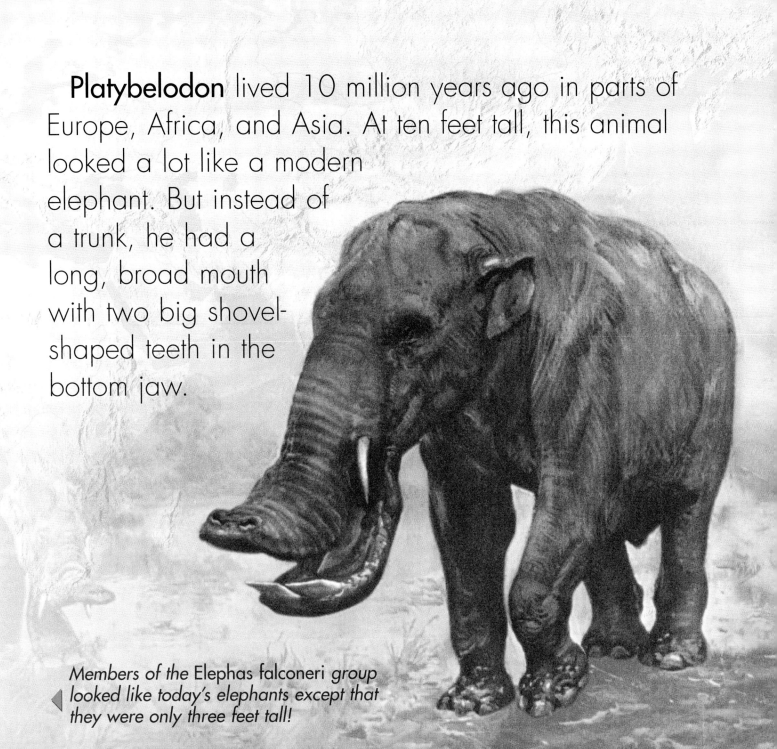

Platybelodon lived 10 million years ago in parts of Europe, Africa, and Asia. At ten feet tall, this animal looked a lot like a modern elephant. But instead of a trunk, he had a long, broad mouth with two big shovel-shaped teeth in the bottom jaw.

Members of the Elephas falconeri group looked like today's elephants except that they were only three feet tall!

MASTODONS

Have you ever heard of a hairy elephant?
The great American mastodon had a coat of long, shaggy hair that protected it from the cold **climate** in which it lived. Even its trunk was furry! This distant relative of today's elephant died out just a few thousand years ago. That means that mastodons lived at the same time as some humans!

Mastodons grew to be ten feet tall. These large creatures lived in Europe, Asia, and all over North America, including what is now the United States.

Mastodons had strong shoulders to hold up their long tusks and heavy heads.

WOOLLY MAMMOTHS

The **woolly mammoth** was another prehistoric relative of the elephant. The mammoth had a long, shaggy coat and a thick wool-like layer of fur underneath. Mammoths were about nine feet tall with high, rounded heads. Unlike the modern elephant, the mammoth had very small ears. Most mammoths died out about 10,000 years ago, but some dwarf mammoths lived on an island off the coast of Siberia until only 4,000 years ago.

The woolly mammoth's huge tusks grew out and then curved inward, sometimes overlapping each other. ▶

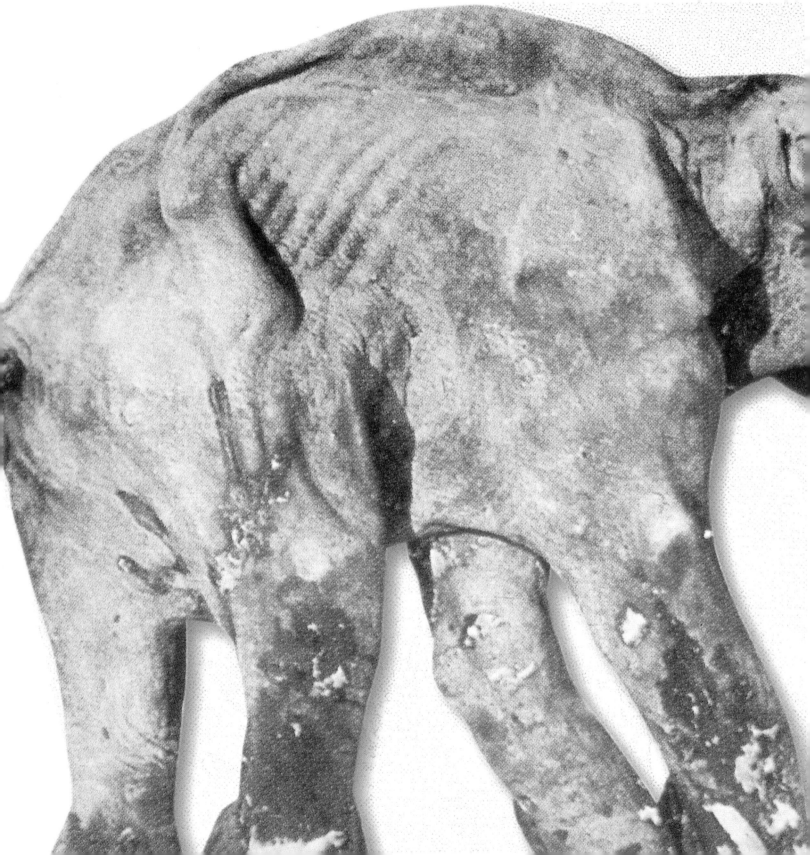

A 40,000-YEAR-OLD BABY

Sometimes the bodies of animals that live in very cold climates freeze in the ground where they die.

In 1977, in the cold land of Siberia, a 40,000-year-old baby mammoth was found frozen in the ground! The people who found her named her Dima.

From studying her **remains**, scientists learned that she was six months old when she died.

You don't have to go all the way to Siberia to find ancient remains. At the Big Bone Lick State Park in Kentucky, thousands of prehistoric bones have been found in a lake. This lake was once a swampy bog that trapped unlucky animals, including mastodons.

It is a lucky break for scientists to find the complete remains of a prehistoric animal. They can learn a lot from such a find.

HUMANS AND THE MAMMOTH

Humans who lived during the time of the mammoths and mastodons were a lot like us. They needed places to live and food to eat. Instead of going to the grocery store to buy their dinner, though, they had to hunt for their food. One favorite meal was mammoth meat. It took several hunters to kill one of these huge animals.

In modern-day France and Spain, you can visit caves where prehistoric people once lived. We think that the mammoth was an important part of their lives because they drew lots of pictures of mammoths on the walls of their caves.

Early people used the mammoth's bones and tusks to make weapons and tools. ▶

ELEPHANTS TODAY

Today, only two species of elephants remain. The African elephant lives south of the Sahara Desert in Africa. The Asian elephant, which is smaller than its African cousin, lives in certain parts of Asia and India.

Elephants can eat as much as 500 pounds of grass, shrubs, twigs and branches a day.

Female elephants and young elephants live in family herds led by a **matriarch**. Grown-up male elephants live alone, or in all-male groups. Elephants are smart and sensitive animals. When an elephant family member dies, the other elephants will often **mourn** the death by touching the dead family member with their trunks.

ELEPHANTS OF YESTERDAY AND TODAY

The elephant-like creatures that lived millions of years ago looked different than the elephants of today. For example, they had furrier bodies and longer tusks. Today's elephants don't share many **characteristics** with their ancient relatives. Modern-day elephants' bodies and features are adapted for today's world. We continue to learn about the elephant-like animals of the past and the elephants of today by studying and respecting these unusual creatures.

WEB SITES:

http://www.museum.state.il.us/exhibits/larson/mammuthus.html

GLOSSARY

adapt (uh-DAPT) To change to fit different conditions.

ancestor (AN-ses-ter) A creature from which others develop.

characteristic (KER-ek-ter-IS-tik) A special quality that separates something from others like it.

climate (KLY-mit) The weather conditions of a place.

Deinotherium (dy-noh-THEER-ee-um) A type of early elephant that lived from about 25 million years ago to 5 million years ago.

dwarf (DWARF) Something that is much smaller than normal.

Elephas falconeri (EL-eh-fus fal-kon-AR-ee) An early dwarf elephant that lived on islands in the Mediterranean Sea.

evolution (eh-vuh-LOO-shun) A slow process of change and development that many living things go through over a long period of time.

extinct (ek-STINKT) To no longer exist.

mammoth (MA-muth) A close prehistoric relative of the modern-day elephant.

mastodon (MAS-tuh-don) A distant prehistoric relative of the elephant.

matriarch (MAY-tree-ark) The female head of a group of elephants.

Moeritherium (mer-eh-THEER-ee-um) The earliest-known elephant-like animal.

mourn (MORN) To show or feel sadness over the death of something.

Platybelodon (plad-ee-BEL-oh-don) A prehistoric relative of the elephant that had huge shovel-shaped teeth.

proboscidean (proh-beh-SID-ee-an) A member of a large group of animals that has a trunk like an elephant.

prehistoric (pree-his-TOR-ik) Existing before recorded history.

remains (re-MAYNZ) What is left of a plant or animal after it has died.

species (SPEE-sheez) A group of plants or animals that are very much alike.

woolly mammoth (WUHL-ee MA-muth) The most famous of the prehistoric mammoths living in North America until about 10,000 years ago.

INDEX